PROFITS FROM YOUR BACKYARD HERB GARDEN

By Lee Sturdivant

Published by SAN JUAN NATURALS
Box 642
Friday Harbor, WA 98250

Art by Peggy Sue McRae
Photos by John Dustrude

PROFITS FROM YOUR BACKYARD HERB GARDEN

By Lee Sturdivant

Published by SAN JUAN NATURALS
Box 642
Friday Harbor, WA 98250
© Copyright 1988
Fourth Edition

ACKNOWLEDGEMENTS

I gladly and sincerely acknowledge the help, encouragement and advice I have received on this first book from the following people: Daniel Poynter; Loren Kaye; Peggy Sue McRae; John Dustrude; Ben Richards; Peter Sturdivant; Jerry Miller; Mary and Smitty Smith; Helen Stegall; Tal Sturdivant, a patient and helpful partner, and Elizabeth McNatt, who made it happen. My thanks to all.

TABLE OF CONTENTS

Welcome to the World of Fresh Green Herbs 7
Planning and Growing 11
Twelve Basic Culinary Herbs 15
Additional Possibilities 40
    Edible Flowers 41
    Mixed Herbs, Greens and Flowers 51
Seed Starting Information 57
Fertilizer and Pesticides 59
Marketing and Business Details 61
    Grocery Marketing 63
    Restaurants 70
    Improving Your Sales 71
    Billing Details 74
    Taxes 77
    Other Business Possibilities 78
Harvesting, Packaging and Kitchen Use 79
    Package and Label 80
    How and How Much to Pick 82
    Herb by Herb Harvesting Hints 85
Afterword 107
Reference Books 109
Plant and Seed Sources 114

WELCOME TO THE WORLD OF FRESH GREEN HERBS

FRESH CUT green herbs have *arrived* in the American kitchen. And they aren't going to go away.

If you're a backyard gardener, you can play a small but profitable part in this change in our food seasoning habits. This book is written to help you turn your home gardening efforts into a paying operation in the fresh herb renaissance.

We're not talking about get rich schemes. We're not talking about million dollar pay-offs. But you'll finish this book knowing exactly how to earn fifty to two-hundred and fifty dollars a week in your spare time, harvesting herbs from an average sized back yard garden planted in culinary herbs.

Just as dried herbs became a real part of our cooking some forty years ago (after WWII) so now have American cooks been "turned on" to using fresh cut herbs in their recipes. And years from now they'll be using even more fresh herbs.

Why? First of all, because fresh herbs make home and restaurant cooking *taste* so much better. And, even more importantly for you, there are strong forces pushing us toward using more fresh herbs in our cooking.

1) **The Gourmet Push:** Pick up any food or household magazine and recipe after recipe extols the "good taste" virtue of fresh cut herbs — with one luscious looking photo after another showing herbs in sauces, herbs in pastas, herbs as garnish, herbs as main ingredients. For the gourmets, fresh herbs are in.

2) **The Salt Free Push:** All the health and fitness magazines, newspaper columns and TV shows now advocate the use of fresh and dried herbs in place of salt, which is now seen as an overused, even dangerous additive which we need to limit in our diets.

3) **The Simplicity Push:** This one runs right alongside (not in contrast to) the Gourmet Push. It urges us to simplify our lives and get back to basics, using less processed foods, fresher and

fresher ingredients. Fresh cut green herbs are always high on these lists, their use encouraged in place of chemical additives.

These are all very powerful forces, and they are helping to change the way we cook and serve our foods. They are very definitely pushing us towards the use of fresh green herbs every day.

A few years ago only the most expensive gourmet markets carried any fresh herbs besides parsley. Now produce people in markets in even the smallest towns, are being asked by their customers for fresh herbs. These are the customers who are reading the cooking magazines, watching the cooking shows, tasting all the new foods in restaurants and then wanting to try those dishes at home. They're asking your neighborhood produce manager for more and more herbs. This book is written to help you fill that market opening as a local supplier of fresh cut herbs to both markets and restaurants.

I began selling herbs quite a few years ago, first as potted plants in farmer's markets, then wholesale to nurseries, and finally as freshly cut green herbs in the local supermarkets.

I've seen my own small business grow and prosper and I know from all I read and hear that the demand for herbs is increasing all over the country. All good produce people want to keep up with food trends; your fresh herbs will be a welcome addition to their produce section IF you learn a few marketing tricks that I will pass along to you.

Fresh herb growing and selling is a small business that takes very little time once you have established a productive garden and can follow a few basic time saving tips.

My herbs in a local market

PLANNING AND GROWING

THIS MARKET garden plan is based on your having only one or two good store accounts; that is, one or two busy stores that sell your herbs. But the plan could also take care of additional smaller stores and a few small restaurants, as they can often fit in nicely around one or two good market accounts. You'll need to grow these amounts of herbs to do the dollar volume ($50.00 to $250.00 per week) this book is aimed at.

If you have the room, you can extend this plan indefinitely, but then you're talking about something more than a small backyard operation. This book is not about row cropping, but small backyard gardens using space very efficiently. For those of you who have the extra room, there's information about going on to a bigger herb selling business. But its primary aim is toward the small, even beginning market gardener. The wonderful thing about herbs in the garden is that they can be fitted in all over the yard, among both flowers and vegetables, all by themselves, under trees, or even in large planters.

I'll tell you the amount of plants to grow plus a little bit about the space requirements, depending on the herb. These gardening suggestions are also written on the assumption that you may already have a flower and/or vegetable garden on your property and that you don't want to give those up.

If you should be able to start these ideas in a new garden, raised beds would definitely be advisable; they are easier to care for and allow the kind of focused intensive gardening this plan aims for. There are lots of books on that subject. (See the reference section at the end of this book.)

In order to keep the start up costs down, and encourage even small space gardeners, I've kept the number of herb plants needed at a minimum. If you have the room and can afford to plant more, feel free to do so; you'll sell all you can grow once your business is established.

My herb gardening effort has been in the Pacific Northwest, in gardening zone 6, where the temperature seldom goes below ten degrees and the summers are cool. You must, of course, adapt this plan to your own environment and weather limitations.

If you live in a severe winter climate area, you'll have a somewhat shorter season, and may even want to consider doing some greenhouse growing. I don't cover greenhouse growing in this book.

If you live in zone 8 or 9, you may do much of your gardening in fall, winter and spring, leaving only a few herbs for the hottest summertime growing.

Please remember that the basic information I give for each plant is for average growing conditions. (A young friend recently questioned my listing the average height of basil at eighteen inches. His lush basil plants reach three and four feet in his backyard . . . which happens to be made up of rich Sacramento River delta soil.)

You don't have to be a gardening expert to get into this business, but every bit of gardening information you learn, especially about your own area, will help you enormously.

If this is your first gardening effort, expect this business to take a year or two to get going well. If you're already growing herbs, you probably just need the marketing and packaging hints to put you in business almost instantly.

BASIL BASICS: *Ocimum basilicum. Annual. Grows to 18". Plant seed indoors in mid-April. Requires dark and 70 degrees temperature to germinate. Germinates in 5 to 10 days. Plant 6" to 8" apart. Needs full sun.*

TWELVE BASIC CULINARY HERBS

T HE HERBS are listed in the order of their importance for marketing. But that can be a little different for each part of the country. Even living in an ethnic neighborhood can make a difference in the popularity of some herbs.

BASIL

If you only have room for one herb — make it basil. If you want to know which herb to allow the most space for, make it basil.

Basil is the herb that has really switched America on to herbs, and this herb has now passed the fad stage and is fast becoming a seasoning staple. Or rather it would be if markets could get enough of it.

So right away make a special place in your garden plan for basil; at least 4' x 10' if you can possibly do it. The plants can be put fairly close together, say 6" to 8" apart. Try to grow at least thirty plants your first year.

I would make at least two plantings of basil, 3 or 4 weeks apart, so that you can harvest it until first frost. Every time I've checked my sales closely, I find that the packages of basil almost always sell first. I'm certain I lose a lot of sales every year just because I don't allow even more space to this popular herb.

You should plant basil seeds; buying enough plants will be too costly. Purchase common or sweet basil seeds, not any of the unusual basils (cinnamon, licorice, holy basil, etc.) You can plant the seeds out in the garden after last frost or, a much better idea, start them indoors early and put them out as the soil warms up after the last frost. See the seed starting information later in the book.

Big Hint: Cover basil seedlings with a plastic tunnel. Your production will be earlier and much bigger. Basil hates cool temperatures, so keep it covered until even the nights are warm in your area.

Plastic covers over basil beds keep it growing faster in spring and early summer. This plastic is reinforced with chicken wire and lasts for years. Any clear plastic helps hold in the heat.

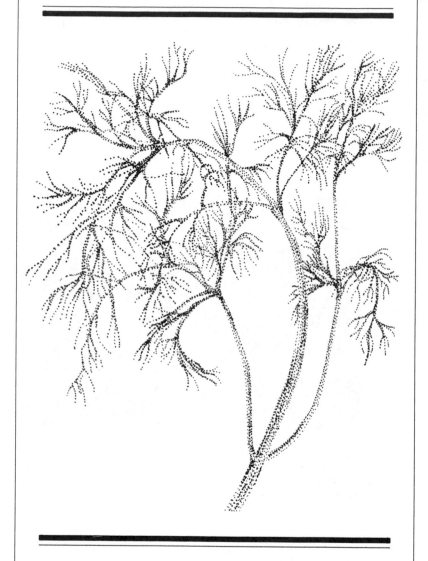

DILL BASICS: *Anethum graveolens. Annual. Bouquet variety grows to 2-1/2 feet. Plant seeds out after last frost. Soil should be 60 degrees. Requires light to germinate. Germination takes 14 days. Thin plants to 8 inches apart. Needs a sunny spot and protection from the wind.*

DILL

The first important point to be made about dill is that there are two types of dill seeds available and you must search out (probably by mail) the ferny or tetraploid dill seeds that are the best for a market herb garden. Ordinary dill, which grows very tall and goes to flower and seed rather quickly, is the best dill for pickling. But it is the lush ferny dill that good cooks want for salads, fish cooking and dips. If you have lots of room, it's fine to grow both kinds of dill. But find the ferny dill and start out with that. (See resource list for seed houses.)

Plant dill two to four times a season, depending on your sales. You need at least twenty to thirty plants each planting. Dill seedlings don't really transplant very well so it's best to plant the seeds just where you want them to grow.

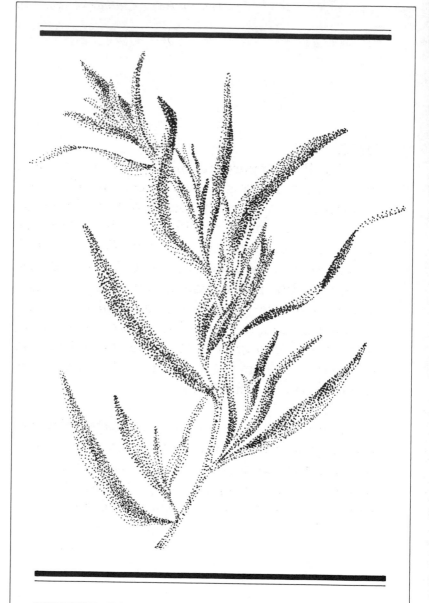

FRENCH TARRAGON BASICS: *Artemesia dracun-culus. Hardy perennial. Cannot be grown from seed. Grows 18" to 24" tall. Spreads. Needs sun and good drainage. Plant starts 12" apart.*

FRENCH TARRAGON

Here's an herb you can't really supply in any quantity for at least a year or two. But it's so valuable for a market herb garden that I'd like to insist that you follow along with my recommendations, put in a good tarragon bed and I know you'll thank me later.

The seeds of the French Tarragon plant are sterile so you must purchase plants. (Don't bother with Russian tarragon seeds — the flavor is not the same at all.) I suggest you start with at least four plants — buy six or eight if you can afford them. Now clear a well drained sunny spot at least 3' x 6' and put your starts in as though they were little cabbage plants; about that far apart.

Tarragon plants lose their leaves in the winter; the first year you'll swear you've lost the plants. Be patient, they'll return in the spring (if they aren't allowed to sit in water during the winter). The little bed will seem to invite weeds, and tarragon and weeds are very incompatible — so keep it weeded all the time. The plants will spread, slowly but surely, and that's what they have to do before you can really start to harvest the precious leaves. I would advise against picking any leaves at all the first year (okay, one tiny taste) and that you pick rather sparingly the second year. By the third year you'll have a strong bed that can last quite a while and pay off year after year. The plants do seem to "wear out" a bit after five or six years when you'll want to start adding new plants into the bed to help rejuvenate it.

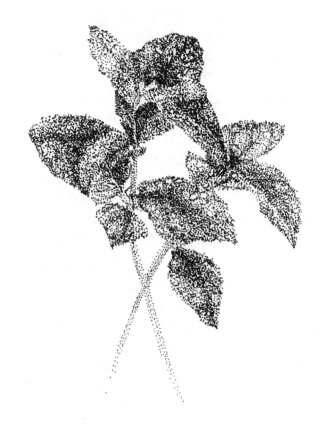

MINT BASICS: *Mentha. Start spearmint from seeds inside at 55 degrees. Seed germinates in 10 to 14 days. Needs light to germinate. Plant 18" apart. Will spread. Buy peppermint starts. Mints are hardy perennials.*

MINTS

Mints take a special place in the garden because they can become so invasive. You may even want to consider planting them in large pots, but if you do, remember that mints take lots of water and can dry out very easily when grown in pots. Pot-grown mints will need watering every day in hot weather, even twice a day.

But mints can grow in shady spots, need little care other than water and are good sellers. If you live in a mild winter area, mints can be grown all year long.

I suggest you start your culinary mint beds with spearmint, which can be grown easily from seeds, and with black peppermint, which you must locate from a nursery. Peppermints seldom come true with seeds. I just make a point of taking a little taste of mint wherever I come upon it and taking home starts of anything that tastes especially good.

You can add other mints as you go along (apple mint, orange mint, pineapple mint etc.) but start off with two or three good plants each of spearmint and peppermint (preferably black.) Keep all mints separate from each other as they can combine and change flavor over seasons of growing into one another. Cut the plants back before they flower and they will produce a whole new crop and spread like crazy.

OREGANO BASICS: *Origanum. Hardy perennial. Seeds can be started inside in winter. Requires dark to germinate. Takes 14 days at 60° temperature. Greek oregano grows about 10" high. Plant 18" apart.*

OREGANO

Most oregano seeds and nursery plants are for a purple flowered variety that grows quite easily and tastes pretty good the first year. But the best culinary variety you must try to find is the white flowered variety called Greek oregano. It has a peppery flavor that good cooks want.

Start with six or eight plants of oregano set in a sunny spot. They do spread a little each year. See the appendix for places to purchase Greek oregano seeds and/or plants.

SWEET MARJORAM BASICS: *Marjorana hortensis.*
*Must be grown as an annual except in completely frost
free zones. Seeds can be started inside at 60°. Needs dark
to germinate. Takes 14 days. Plant in full sun 12" apart.
Grows 12" to 18" tall.*

SWEET MARJORAM

It's important that you learn the difference between oregano and sweet marjoram; closely related but quite different culinary herbs. (Many people mix these up.) Sweet marjoram is the one with stems of knotted flowers. Oregano is the better seller in markets, is winter hardy and more well known. But sweet marjoram is a distinctively delicious herb, very popular wherever lamb is served, and is easily sold to French restaurants.

Plant your seeds inside in winter or early spring and put them out after all frost is gone; six or eight plants will do. They must be planted every year. There is a "winter hardy" marjoram variety that herb nurseries occasionally have, but I've found it to be a little bitter. I grow new marjoram every year.

FRENCH SORREL BASICS: *Rumex scutatus and rumex acetosa. Hardy perennial. Grows 12" tall. Plant 12" apart. Requires 10 days to germinate at 65 degrees.*

FRENCH SORREL

Here's an herb that's growing in popularity and is quite easy to grow and take care of. Be sure to buy French Sorrel *(rumex scutatus* or *rumex ascetosa)* seeds or plants. Start with six plants.

One big problem with sorrel (which grows in partial shade) is that slugs and snails adore it. So you may have to use some bait nearby or keep after the snails and slugs every evening when they can be seen.

Sorrel sends up thick flower stalks all the time; keep these pulled or picked off to encourage more tender leaf growth.

Plant sorrel plants a foot apart, and they will need dividing every couple of years. These plants do best in cool weather.

ROSEMARY BASICS: *Rosemarinus officinalis. Hardy to approximately 10 degrees. Seeds germinate slowly (up to 21 days at 60 degrees in the light) and sparsely (sometimes only 10%.) Plant in full sun and be prepared to protect in the winter. Plant 2' to 3' apart. Rosemary can grow up to 3' tall.*

ROSEMARY

This is one of the few main culinary herbs that may need a little winter protection where temperatures drop below 10 or 15 degrees. I have seen rosemary plants survive below that temperature but, after losing several plants, I now give mine some winter protection. Choose carefully where to put your rosemary; give it your most protected sunny garden spot, even building a little cloche for it if necessary. In severe winter areas, grow it in pots and bring them indoors in winter. Rosemary can be started from seed, but it is so slow growing that I'd definitely recommend buying plants, three or four, to start. It will probably be quite a while before you can sell whole packets of rosemary (unless you live in a Mediterranean climate) but you can sell a very popular mix (see p. 89) the first year using small bits of rosemary.

There are many different varieties of rosemary, but stay with the standard variety *(Rosemarinus officinalis)* to start.

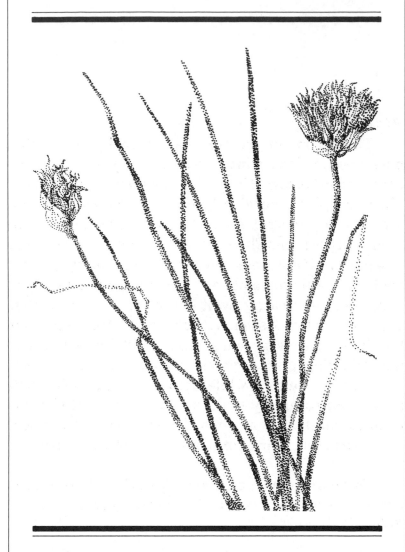

CHIVES BASICS: *Allium schoenoprasum. Perennial clumps, easily grown from seed, started indoors in winter or earliest spring. Seeds take 10 days to germinate at 60 degrees. Plants do well in sun or partial shade. Grow two feet apart and divide every year.*

CHIVES

These are very easy plants to grow and you can even get quite a bit of production the first year if you plant seeds early enough. Starts will give you an even faster crop; I'd suggest 8 to 10 plants to start. Chives need dividing almost every year so you'll end up with quite a lot of them before too long.

Chives are wonderful to grow in the flower garden; their lilac flowers are lovely (and quite edible.) Dried and freeze-dried chives taste so bland compared to fresh ones that you'll find easy acceptance of your garden grown chives in both markets and restaurants.

Newly divided chives, starting to grow again

PARSLEY BASICS: *Petroselinum crispum. Hardy biennial. Soak seeds in hot water before planting. Seeds can take up to 21 days to germinate at 70 degrees. Partial shade okay. Needs lots of moisture. Plant 8" to 10" apart.*

PARSLEY

I'm not suggesting you supply parsley to supermarkets (although I've done a bit of that) but the mixed herb packets that sell so well (see p. 89) need parsley in them and it's best to have a good supply on hand.

Buy one of the very curly varieties and, if you grow it from seed (which is quite easily done) be patient and start early. The seeds can take up to 3 weeks to germinate. Cover the seed with hot water for a few minutes before planting and then plant them in pots in mid-winter and keep them warm and covered. (See the seed germination paragraphs at the end of this section.)

Parsley is a biennial, but you need to plant every year because last year's parsley usually goes to seed rather early the following season. So plant parsley seeds every mid-winter. I usually grow six to eight plants as there are so many uses for it in the kitchen.

If you keep parsley in the same place in your garden year after year, it will eventually seed itself so well you may not have to keep adding new plants. But these seedlings may not be as vigorous as starting new seeds or starts.

THYME BASICS: *Thymus. A perennial that is hardy in all but the most severe winters, where it must be mulched. Seeds germinate in the dark in 14 to 20 days at 70 degrees. Plants need full sun and grow 12" high.*

THYME

There are scores of varieties of this tasty little herb, but the culinary varieties are sold as French, English or Garden thyme. Any of these are fine. Some of the more exotic varieties are also good for kitchen use but you can try those later on for your own kitchen. I do get some requests for lemon thyme, but not a lot.

Thyme plants grow like miniature shrubs with tiny leaflets all over them and little pale flowers in summer (which the bees adore.)

You'll need six thyme plants in a sunny spot and they'll need replacing about every three years as they get very woody. Replace one or two each year so your production won't stop.

SAGE BASICS: *Salvia officinalis. A very hardy perennial, sage grows at least two feet tall. It grows rather easily from seeds or starts. Seeds germinate in 14 days at 65 degrees. Sage requires full sun for growing.*

SAGE

Only one or two sage plants are necessary in your garden. They grow fairly large in a sunny spot and although not a big seller on its own, sage is a necessary addition to the Scarborough Mix, which sells very well.

I also grow several other types of sage (fruit, pineapple, silver etc.) because the flavors are intriguing and the flowers are outstanding. I seldom sell anything besides *salvia officinalis,* or sometimes golden sage, which flowers less and keeps looking good while the regular sage is blooming. Sage can become woody and need replacing after four or five years.

ADDITIONAL POSSIBILITIES

THE PREVIOUS twelve herbs make up my basic culinary herb business, but following is a list of other herbs and plants you may want to add to your herb garden. They can often be sold, usually in smaller amounts than the basic twelve. Perhaps some of these can become important in your area markets. The more herbs you learn to grow and use, the more market opportunities you can find. Look over this list and try to add some of these to your garden. You can find detailed growing information about them in the many herb gardening books now on the market. I'm also including information on edible flowers, one of my best selling items right now.

CHERVIL. A delicious herb, but it bolts easily when the weather warms up and requires constant replanting. I swear every year that I'll give more time and patience to chervil, but I never do. A main ingredient for *fines herbes*.

CILANTRO (Coriander leaves). An important green herb in any area where Mexican or Chinese food is popular. But it takes so many plants to make up an herb packet of cilantro and the plant itself goes so readily to seed, that I've found it to be just too much trouble to grow for market (although I grow it for my own kitchen use.) For some of you, this can definitely become a major herb. Try it in your area.

SUMMER SAVORY. This is easily grown but still not a popular herb in my area. I do sell a little of it each season. The winter savory is even less well known. Savory is an herb you may get requests for from chefs.

FENNEL. I grow bronze fennel and always sell a few packets of it. Fennel is quite delicious with fish but not yet very well known or used in most areas. Some chefs will appreciate it. Green or bronze fennel is easily grown in partial shade.

ELEPHANT GARLIC. A mild yet distinctive flavor. I'm starting to see this garlic more and more often in markets. It's easy to grow but a little expensive to get started with. (See appendix for sources.)

SHALLOTS. If you have the extra room in your garden, shallots can be a real addition to your sales. Grow the true French shallots; they have a slightly purple tinged flesh. There are several other types but these are still the most well known among good cooks.

LOVAGE. One of my own personal favorites. A strong celery taste, it makes a wonderful pesto and some chefs in my area use it constantly. Easily grown. Try to introduce it to your area.

EDIBLE FLOWERS. This is currently a fairly big item for me because I also grow and sell cut flowers. (I'm planning to write a book on cut flower sales next.)

Edible flowers are one of the little gourmet indulgences started in the 80's and now many restaurants all over the country are serving edible flowers. Few chefs are using them as actual recipe ingredients (although that's very possible); but primarily as a garnish. Their customers are told that the flowers are edible, so it's important that they be edible, even though they are seldom eaten. Sounds a little silly, doesn't it?

This is probably a food fad that, unlike fresh herbs, will not remain popular in gourmet restaurants. But if you can do some business in your area while it remains "in", here's some information to help you sell edible flowers.

First of all, the list of edible, that is non-toxic, good tasting flowers is quite limited. There are some very lovely, very poisonous blossoms, so you must take these lists seriously and deliver only what you know to be safe and edible.

Secondly, flower blossoms will not stay fresh nearly as long as freshly cut herbs, so you must take a little extra care with them in order to snip them just before delivery and to keep them cool, very cool, as soon as they are cut.

As of this writing, I even sell a few packets of edible flowers in my markets, but the main sales are primarily to restaurants who like to send out every entre or dessert plate with a little pansy or English daisy or nasturtium on it.

For market sales you can use the regular plastic bags with a couple of dozen blossoms in it. For the restaurants, I am much more selective with the flowers. I put them in little covered plastic bowls so they won't be crushed in big restaurant coolers. See the photos for both of these packing methods.

You can probably buy a few dozen plastic bowls from your neighborhood deli; the kind they use for take-out food. You will have to pay five to twenty cents for each of them, but it would save your having to buy a case. I charge seven cents per flower blossom through a restaurant distributor; I would probably charge ten cents per blossom directly. (More about restaurant distributors later.) I sell the little market packets for $1.00, just like the herbs, but they are not as carefully selected or cared for.

For the restaurants, place a little damp paper towel in the bottom of the plastic bowl, take the bowl to the garden and carefully choose perfect blossoms (not bug eaten or fading) and place them face up in the bowl. I put two dozen blossoms in each bowl and always add a few extra in case some wilt too quickly. At seven cents per blossom you can be a little generous once you have lots of blossoms. Cover the bowl, quickly place it in your refrigerator and deliver the bowls as soon as possible.

I've been looking into edible flowers for a couple of years and what follows is a list of the blossoms that I've learned are edible. Most of the information comes from books (see the bibliography) and from chefs who use them in their cooking.

You can probably add to the list as you go along, but please do so carefully. You can check with your local county agricultural agent or the botany department of a nearby university if you want to know about a specific plant.

I'm also including a list of toxic blossoms that must be avoided.

The market packet, left, goes in with the herbs in the produce section. The plastic bowl is needed for restaurant sales, and more protection.

Edible Blossoms

Borage. *Borago officinalis.* It grows very easily in my area, reseeding itself with abandon. The flowers are tiny but a perfect color and shape. I often sprinkle a few in each edible flower package without charge. If selling them specifically, I'd charge 1½ or 2 cents each. I have had specific orders for them.

Bergamot. *Monarda didyma.* Beebalm. Lovely colors and a good shape if picked early enough in the bloom. These can sometimes run a little too large for use as a garnish. The best blossom size is 1" to 2". 1½" is perfect.

Calendula. *Calendula officinalis.* Pot Marigold. Used in cooking as a saffron substitute; the petals are removed from the calyx or green cup holding the petals. These are good for edible flower sales if they are only 1½" across.

Carnations. *Dianthus.* I sell both carnation flowers and "pinks", the little clove scented varieties whose fragrant flowers are just over an inch across. Only the petals are edible; most blossoms are bitter tasting near the calyx.

Chrysanthemum. *Chrysanthemum morifolium.* All chrysanthemum recipes call for the petals to be removed, but I do sell any small (under 2") blossoms in my edible flower packets.

Citrus blossoms. If you have lemon, lime or orange trees, these fragrant little blossoms are a great addition to a flower blossom packet. I count them as two or three for one, and I grow them in my greenhouse.

Daylilies. *Hemerocallis.* Usually too large to use, but I've started growing miniatures as border plants and the little flowers are a perfect size to sell.

English Daisy. *Bellis perennis.* Sometimes too small the first year but often a nice size the second year.

Fuchsia. Not all that tasty, but certainly lovely as a garnish. I often include one on the top of the other blossoms in the plastic bowl.

Geranium. *Pelargonium.* Not the perennial variety known as Cranesbill,but the common, everyday variety we all call geranium. They are hardy in only a few zones, needing protection most places. But the blossoms, especially the fancier double and large blossom varieties are fine. The blossoms are usually in clusters. Each blossom should be separated to sell.

Gladiolus. Only the small variety is applicable here. Once again, not too tasty but very effective as a garnish.

Hollyhock. *Althaea rosea.* Try to find the dwarf variety. The regular ones are just too large.

Lavender. *Lavandula vera.* I use just the 2 or 3 inch stem end. The fragrance is delightful.

The flowers can be stripped off the stem and used in salads, etc.

Lilac. *Syringa.* Count a small cluster of opened blossoms as one flower blossom. Very welcome in early spring.

Marigold. *Tagates.* These are all pretty bad tasting to me except for the little "Lemon Gem" which has tasty flowers and greens.

Nasturtiums. *Tropaeolum majus.* One of the basics for an edible garden. The peppery tasting leaves are nice in salads, too. I usually include a few leaves in the bowl just for fun. Nasturtiums and pansies are the basic flowers needed for this venture. The others primarily add a little interest.

Pansy & Viola. *Viola hortensis* and *v. cornuta.* Pleasant tasting, delightful to look at and just the right size wanted by the restaurants. Isn't it nice that they are also such fun to have in the garden? Grow lots of them.

Rose. *Rosa.* These truely are interesting to use in the kitchen. But I suggest you grow the miniatures for blossoms to sell. The regular roses are too large, although I do use rosebuds when I have a lot of small ones.

Squash Blossoms. These you can sell in your market packets; many cooks like to stuff them with cheese and saute them after dipping in batter. Fill the whole packet with them. Only take the male blossoms, though; the female blossoms will have tiny fruits attached.

Toxic Blossoms

If you are able to market edible flowers, you should realize how very specific these blossom recommendations are; all flowers are not edible.

Following is a list of toxic or poisonous flower blossoms you may very well have in your garden. It is by no means complete. So take care.

Autumn crocus. *Colchicum autumnale.*
Columbine. *Aquilegia vulgaris.*
Foxglove. *Digitalis purpurea.*
Fritillaria. *Fritillary meleagris.*
Hydrangea. *Hydrangea macrophylla.*
Iris. *Iris foetidissima.*
Lily of the valley. *Convallaria majalis.*
Monkshood. *Aconitum napellus.*
Oleander. *Nerium oleander.*
Poppies. *Papaver.*
Rhododendron. *Rhododendron ponticum.*
Stonecrop. *Sedum acre.*
St. John's wort. *Hypericum perforatum.*
Yellow jessamine. *Gelsemium sempervirens.*

MIXED HERBS, GREENS & FLOWERS

This is the latest addition to my sales and I think it's going to be a good one. There seems to be great interest these days in unusual salad ingredients, so this is a little packet of mixed ingredients that someone can take home, chop up and add to a plain green salad; it immediately jazzes up that salad.

This may require that you grow a few unusual salad greens, but you can use sorrel, lovage and parsley as the basic greens to begin with; green herbs you'd be growing for the basic garden. It's the addition of mixed herbs and flowers that is intriguing to customers and I suggest you try some of this in your own salad bowl first to get the idea.

If you have the room and want to try this idea, grow a few of the following salad greens:

Chicory. There are many interesting varieties of this plant, one of which, *radicchio*, is all the rage now. *Radicchio* is really just the Italian name for red-leaf chicories.

Endive. Another group of chicory-like greens, a little bitter to some people, but a few leaves add great interest to a salad.

Cabbage & Kale. The ornamental versions (very leafy) are good to grow for these little green packets; and easy to grow, too.

Oriental Greens: Pak choi, Chinese cabbage, oriental mustard.

Chard. Either the green or red variety is fine.

Plus, of course, all the many different types of lettuce now available by seed or from starts.

I'll tell you a couple of combinations I use in the mixed packets but only because they're available, not because they necessarily go well together. Try your own combinations based on what you can grow. Try them first in your own salads and then go from there.

Mixed Greens Packet

Sometimes I add the words "For Salads" on this label. A fuchsia blossom and nasturtium blossom are near the top.

Combination #1. Several leaves of chicory, lovage and purple ornamental cabbage, plus two or three stems each of oregano, chervil, basil, plus three or four stems of chives plus four to eight edible flower blossoms: perhaps lemon gem marigolds, chive blossoms, a couple of pansies or a miniature rose.

Combination #2. Several leaves of sorrel, *radicchio,* and plain or curled parsley; two or three stems each of bronze fennel, tarragon and dill, plus edible flowers such as English daisies, *pelargoniums* and *dianthus.*

To make your test salad at home, wash and dry some leafy lettuce or romaine and chop or tear the pieces into the salad bowl.

Then wash and dry the packet of mixed greens, herbs and flowers (a salad spinner is a great help here) and chop them rather finely and sprinkle them into the salad.

I like a basic vinaigrette dressing made with good olive oil, vinegar or lemon juice, mustard, salt and pepper and a pinch of sugar. Pour the dressing over the salad and mix well and serve. Yum.

One key trick in making wonderful salads is to take the time to dry the ingredients carefully (so the dressing isn't carried away by the water left on the leaves).

Heating cable and hardware cloth

Starting seeds in pots over heat

SEED STARTING INFORMATION

THE KEY points I'd like to make to novice seed planters are: 1) Add bottom heat to seeds and 2) Keep them moist.

I grow seeds in three ways:

1. In little moistened peat pellets (size 9) put in small trays or plastic egg cartons. After wetting the pellets (they increase in height) put two or three seeds in each pellet. I then put a little piece of hardware cloth over a small heating cable (available in garden centers and hardware stores) and put the trays or egg cartons on top of the hardware cloth. That protects the cartons from melting.

Cover each tray or egg carton with plastic wrap after they are planted. That will keep the seeds moistened until germination. Check the seeds every day or so to see if they are germinating, and as soon as most seeds do, remove the plastic wrap and move the plants into good light. They can remain in the peat pellets for at least a few weeks if you keep them well watered. They can then be potted up into 4"-6" pots or put into the garden if the time is right for planting out.

This method is handy when you only want to end up with a few plants of one kind.

2. The same method can be used for small pots, using very damp potting soil to within ½" of the top. Add the seeds, cover with plastic wrap and place over a heating cable as above.

3. When you want to grow a lot of one plant (as with basil) use a shallow plastic or wooden tray filled with very damp potting soil. Be certain there are drainage holes in the tray. Sprinkle on the seeds, then add a thin covering of soil. Cover with plastic wrap and place the tray over the hardware cloth and heating cable. After the seeds have germinated, remove the wrap (which keeps the moisture in) put the tray in good light and let the plants grow until they get at least four good leaves. Then transplant into 2" or 4" pots where they can remain until the weather is good for planting out. For basil, in zone 6, I plant the seeds indoors in March and put the plants outside (covered with plastic) in mid to late May, or even June, depending on the weather.

FERTILIZER AND PESTICIDES

HERBS ARE rather easily grown plants with few problems. I use compost in my garden and spread chicken manure laden sawdust from chicken barns through my gardens once a year. I never see the need to use commercial fertilizers on the herbs.

Herbs that have been sprayed with insecticides seem unsaleable to me. I sell unwashed herbs so that they'll stay fresher longer in the packets. I wouldn't want to sell herbs covered with poisons. I do have to use slug bait near the sorrel bed, but otherwise it's better to sell organically grown herbs and to advertise them as such on your label. Organically grown food is certainly what health conscious people are demanding more and more of these days, so why not start out your herb business that way to begin with.

MARKETING AND BUSINESS DETAILS

Getting into Business

Do you live in a town or county that requires a business license? Does your state require a resale number in order to do business? Will you have a zoning problem by growing commercial crops in your garden?

If you've never been in business, all these questions may seem very serious and difficult; like obstacles in your way. But there are a couple of things to remember here before you get too worried over "the legalities."

#1 The Tax laws, and most other laws, favor small businesses. All the red tape you hear and read about constantly concern large and medium size businesses; those the government is trying to keep track of and work with on one thing and another. The business we are talking about is so small as to be nearly invisible. Small and straight forward; you won't have a lot of red tape to deal with.

#2 Retail business people often collect sales taxes for their state, county and or town. These are retail sales taxes. You will be selling your herbs wholesale. Wholesale selling means that you always sell to someone who sells to the public; either a grocer or a restaurant. The wholesaler (or grower) does not charge or collect sales taxes. That is done at the retail level only.

Your state, county or town may charge you a Fee or License to do business, but you don't collect or pay sales taxes for or to them as long as you only sell wholesale.

I operate under a town license for $42.00 per year and have a low-cost state business/tax number, called a Resale Number, that allows me to make business purchases at wholesale. I pay state sales taxes on books sold by mail order in my own state.

Those are the only licenses, business taxes and fees that I have had to contend with in five years of business.

Your state, county and/or town fees may be a little different, of course, but they won't amount to much. To find out the business licensing agency of your state, look at the state license posted in any store. The agency name will be there. Give them a call.

Call your town or county office, and ask them about licenses needed for operating a small business. One person who can be so much help to you in all of this is your county agricultural agent. The same rules will apply to you in selling herbs to your grocer as would apply if you were selling zucchini or rhubarb to your grocer. The county agricultural agents have a wealth of information; give them a call if you can't quite figure out how to start.

As far as zoning is concerned, the same kind of wholesale versus retail thinking applies: if you're dealing with retail customers, zoning really counts. Neighborhoods can get up in arms about a small business setting up in a residential area if there are customers coming and going all the time. But you're going to be taking your herbs to market; there'll be no zoning problems at all.

MARKETING

I am always amazed at how intimidated people are by the idea of marketing or selling anything they produce. They imagine there's an impossibly high wall between what goes on in the front of a grocery store and what goes on in back, where they never feel welcome.

The people who *are* welcome in the back of the store are the people with something good to sell. And that's what you'll have with fresh green herb packets.

What follows is a step by step method to sell your herbs after your herb garden is producing at least 4 herbs in decent quantities. Read it over several times before you start out to sell. It should help you with those first steps, which are always the hardest. After that you'll probably improve on my system and go on from there.

Pick your stores carefully. You'll want a busy store, but don't start with the big chains. (More about that later.) Look for a store with signs of being successful at what they're doing. Look over their produce section and ask yourself: Are these grocers trying hard to reach the good cooks in this area? Is there a large refrigerated produce section? This is very important, as fresh cut herbs are most like lettuce or spinach and must be constantly refrigerated to remain crisp and fresh.

You only need a *few* stores; even one or two can sell a lot of herbs, but you want to find the best ones for your product.

You're going to be a small but high quality supplier so it's important that you not spread yourself too thin, especially to start. Don't put your herbs in marginal stores, those that seem to be having a hard time staying open, or are really just a small addition to gasoline sales or something like that. Most convenience stores (like 7 Eleven) don't have real produce sections; they are not good ones to chose.

After you've chosen a market, look to see if they are already selling fresh herbs. If they are, find out if the herbs are supplied locally. Usually the herbs will be labelled showing where they come from. If they are local and there's a good selection, move on to another store for your first account. It's best to start your business with all the advantages, and trying to displace someone who's already doing a good job is not an advantage.

But if the herbs are from hundreds or thousands of miles away, you can offer the store a real advantage if they switch to your herbs.

So now you have picked out your first target store. Then you must find out the produce buyer's name and the hours during which they can be seen. You can get that information at the store or from home on the phone.

Make an early morning appointment to see them to show them "a locally grown product you know they'll like."

Now prepare at least two or three packets of your garden fresh herbs to show. (See the Chapter on Harvesting and Preparation.) It's a thousand times better to take in fresh herb packets than just to go in and talk about them. Most buyers get too many people coming in to tell what they can do IF the buyer will promise to buy a lot. Showing your herbs is the very best way to get an order.

The Spiel.

Your greengrocer is most interested in a few things when considering a new product: Having a good selection of products to keep the customers coming in *and* making a decent profit on them without a big loss in unsold waste. You must now offer that greengrocer all of the above.

"I grow these kitchen herbs in my back yard. I'm prepared to keep you supplied in fresh culinary herbs, take back any packets that don't sell and try to meet any special needs your customers might have.

"I get one dollar for each packet that sells. Most stores charge $1.49 for the packet and I can bill you weekly or monthly.

"I'll check the display at least twice a week. I'm reliable and eager to make my little herb business grow."

That's the basic information you need to get across. Read it over and over until you know exactly what to say. Be straight forward and good humored and don't waste his time with small talk. You'll have a chance to get acquainted later as you do business there. But produce people are very, very busy in the best markets and expect you to be business-like in your dealings with them.

This basic spiel is all the selling you have to do to get into the herb business. If you've chosen the right market, you'll find that getting the account is not a problem. Produce people these days know that herbs are becoming big business because their customers are asking for them.

Now let's take a look at just what you've offered and are asking for in return.

First of all, you're not asking for an order for so many packets of such and such an herb. That's not the best way for a backyard grower to market herbs. You want to keep as much control as possible in this little business and that means being able to sell just what you have that's ready to harvest. In most weather zones you can supply some herbs from May to October, but not all varieties that whole time. In some zones you can supply almost all year around. These days your sales will always be highest during the basil season, but other herbs, like dill and tarragon for instance, are becoming very, very popular, too.

What you're really wanting is to rent a tiny little space on your greengrocer's refrigerated counter where you can keep the market supplied with something they and their customers want. By offering to take back any packets that don't sell, you can also control your sales because you'll know exactly what to offer and can monitor the sales very well. Often grocers can order the "wrong" items, then when they don't sell, the grocer takes the loss and the supplier doesn't get any more business. You can take the first losses, learn from your customers and continue to supply what they want. This point is very important. You want to decide just what to bring into market.

The 49 cent mark-up is really quite generous but your grocer is free to mark it up higher if he wants to — he knows what his customers will pay. The dollar fee to you should remain steady. That's what makes all the work worthwhile. (For information on weights and amounts, see the chapter on Harvesting and Preparation.)

So now you have your first good account. Before you go dashing off to sell to Store #2, take time to learn how to service #1 and turn it into a well paying account. Here are some suggestions to follow in taking care of that first store.

After the grocer agrees to try your herbs:

1) Take in at least 15 or 20 packets for your first delivery.

2) Take your first order in in a nice basket so that in case the store doesn't have a small tray for the refrigerated counter you can leave the basket. Herbs look great in a basket and sell very well from one. Just be sure it stays in the refrigerated section.

3) Take along a small sign, *"Local Fresh Herbs."*. You can attach it to the basket or the display until the market gets around to making their own. Make your sign as waterproof as possible as water sprays are often used over the whole refrigerated section.

4) Offer to price your own packets. Sometimes a store will appreciate the help in marking; other stores will just have you leave the herbs in the back until an employee has time to mark them.

5) Be certain to have an employee sign for each delivery. (See Business Details for more on this.)

6) To start with, keep a separate tally of what you take in so that you can learn what's selling the fastest. Bring in not less than six packets of herbs per delivery. Remove any packets that start

looking unappetizing. If the herbs are packaged correctly and kept in the refrigerated section, they should hold up fine for about a week — some for much longer.

Don't get discouraged if the sales are slow to start. Customers have to get to used to seeing a new vegetable or fruit or greens. You may even lose money for the first few weeks, but if you've chosen the right store and grown fine herbs, you'll soon start selling lots of packets and decide it's time to look for a second account. Be certain your garden will produce enough now to more than double your sales. It may be you'll want to stay with just one market the first season, until your garden is producing more.

Now, what about those chain stores? Yes, definitely consider them, especially if there are no good local owner stores in your area. But your sales method may have to be quite different. Many, but not all, large chains forbid their produce managers from buying local crops. Your produce manager will tell you this when you go in to see him. But show him your packets and ask if he'd like to carry them if you go to the trouble of going to the main office. If he's interested, it may be worth your while to go further. Those buying offices may be a long way away, even a hundred miles or so. I've never felt the additional expense would be worth it. I have always found that it's easier to look harder for small specialty stores, delis, or locally owned grocers. While your first herb crops are growing, take your time in finding just the right first account.

RESTAURANTS

Restaurants are a golden opportunity for a backyard herb dealer. Pick out the gourmet restaurants in your area, or more to the point, those restaurants that feature lots of fresh vegetables, specialty salads, home made soups and breads.

By phone you can find out the name of the chef and what time she comes to work. Try to see the chef as early in the day as possible. Like the greengrocer, chefs are very busy people. Use the same spiel you do for markets, but of course chefs won't be reselling your packets directly. Take in two or three packets to start, keep your price at $1, leave the packets with her to try (no charge) and call back in a day or two to see if you can do business there.

You may find that one or two restaurants plus one good market account can use up your fresh herb supply quite nicely, especially the first year or two. After your garden is well established and you know just what to expect from your plants (and have probably added to your inventory based on your own sales) you can reach out to all sorts of new accounts. But meanwhile, here are some hints on improving sales in the store account you already have.

IMPROVING YOUR SALES

One of the very best ways to improve your market sales is to arrange to do a food demonstration at the market that sells your herbs. This is an easy way to increase your sales for the short term and also familiarize the customers with the taste of fresh herbs.

One important note here: Be certain that during the time you are learning how to grow and sell culinary herbs that you are also learning to use them in your own home kitchen. You will be asked endless questions about cooking with herbs as you become involved in their selling; make sure you learn enough about their use to speak intelligently and give recommendations to consumers eager to try these new flavors in their recipes.

I recommend several herb cook books in the bibliography, and offer at least one recipe per herb in the harvesting chapter. I want to encourage you to work with herbs in your kitchen every day. You will become more enthusiastic about these magical green plants as you use them.

To give a food demonstration in your market, you agree on a day and time with a produce manager (usually a Friday or Saturday afternoon when the market is certain to be busy) and you set up a small table covered with a colorful tablecloth, near the produce department.

One very easy and good tasting tid-bit for an herb demonstration is herb-cheese stuffed celery bites. Blend chopped green herbs with low-fat cottage cheese or yoghurt and then stuff tiny bits of celery and serve from a plate in the market. The celery is bland enough to let the herb flavor come through and makes a fine little holder.

You need to experiment a little with this at home to get something you like and that you know will taste good to others. Tarragon, basil, chives or oregano; use herbs you have in quantity as you'll sell a lot of those.

Food demonstrations are a wonderful way for you to learn about your customers; they will engage you in endless conversations (keep giving out samples to other customers as you chat.) Take along some tiny paper napkins, a waste basket, a plate for serving, a cutting board and knife. The market will sell or give you the celery and a place to wash and cut it up. Cut up a lot before you start, stash it in a plastic bag and put it in the store's refrigerator section until you need it.

Often a store will expect a discount on the product sold that day — say 85 cents instead of a dollar a packet for that one day only, and they mark down the herbs for the customer, too. I'd agree to this, but only if asked. Don't volunteer to give anything away.

Another way to increase sales in markets is to supply little herb recipe cards near your display.

Type your favorite herb recipe (be sure you have plenty of that herb on hand) on an 8½ x 11 sheet, making 6 or 8 copies of the recipe on the one sheet. Make 10 or 12 copies of the sheet and then cut out the recipes with a paper cutter (or scissors.) Finally, staple the stack of 80 or 100 recipes to a cardboard backing and take them to the greengrocer to put up near your herbs. Again, make sure you do this when you have a lot of the herb on hand that you're featuring in the recipe. Feel free to use my recipes.

Make friends at the delis and restaurants you think might be interested in using your fresh herbs. I once supplied a recipe and a bowl of sorrel soup to a small restaurant that seemed anxious to serve very fresh food and please their customers. The owner was delighted and served sorrel soup for months using my sorrel.

Who teaches cooking classes in your area? They will be interested in using your herbs and they can tell their students where to get your herbs.

I also sell herbs through a fruit and vegetable distributor who deals only with restaurants. He took around packets of my herbs to his accounts and now calls in his orders to me once or twice a week.

You can sell lots of fresh herb packets at a Saturday or Farmer's Market. Be sure to take along a tub of ice to display them in (out of the sun!) and don't undercut yourself if your market account is nearby. If your market account is quite some distance away, sell your herbs at the Farmer's market for one dollar a packet. When your have lots of basil, dill and French tarragon, you can make many sales.

These are just a few of the ideas I have used over the years to increase my own sales. I hope they'll lead you to even better ideas for your growing business.

BILLING DETAILS

One of the first things to do is order a rubber stamp with your company name (keep it simple) address and telephone number on it. You'll need this for your invoices. It could also be used on your first labels.

At your local office supply or drugstore you can buy a book of duplicate invoices. In my area, they come in a little blue colored book of fifty sets for just over two dollars.

Use your rubber stamp across the top of the original copy (which the store will end up keeping) and insert the carbon paper behind that first sheet to make a copy for your records.

Each invoice can be used for 4 to 8 deliveries to one store or restaurant. (See the attached example.)

The important thing to remember is to have someone who works at the business sign for each and every delivery. Have them sign their name or initial along the day's delivery line instead of at the bottom of the invoice.

After a few deliveries, I add up the column on the right and turn in the invoice to the produce manager, chef or bookkeeper.

Many stores and restaurants will want to pay you immediately, either with a check or cash out of the cash drawer. For those who want credit, I always show terms on the Invoice as, "Net 10 Days" meaning I expect to be paid the full amount within 10 days.

One word of warning: I would be a little more careful about extending credit to small restaurants (especially if they're rather new) than to markets. Don't be afraid to say, "I'm the world's smallest company, and need to keep my money coming in while I get started. Please pay me weekly."

The easiest way to handle any take-backs is to subtract them from your delivery total. If you take in 24 fresh herb packets and pick up three unsold ones that look unappetizing, charge for 21 packets on your invoice entry for that day.

This is the simplest, yet adequate, billing method you can use to start out with. You don't need to send additional statements. If your store hasn't paid you in 10 to 20 days, go in and talk with them. Monthly statements are an additional expense you don't need. Keep in close touch with

SAN JUAN NATURALS
Box 642
Friday Harbor, WA 98250
378-2648

INVOICE NO. **2149**

SOLD TO	Kings Market
STREET & NO.	Spring St.
CITY	Friday Harbor STATE Wa. ZIP 98250

SHIPPED TO
STREET & NO.
CITY   STATE   ZIP

CUSTOMER'S ORDER	SALESMAN	TERMS	F.O.B	DATE

SALESMAN: Jennifer Rogers
TERMS: Net 10 days

Date		Qty			
9/21/87	18 packets	1.00	18.00
9/24/87	24 packets	1.00	24.00
9/28/87	17 packets	1.00	17.00
10/1/87	25 packets	1.00	25.00
			$84.00

INVOICE

Here's an example of a simple invoice for a store account. Use a rubber stamp at the top. Using one line per delivery, you can do 4 to 8 deliveries with one invoice.

your accounts, not letting them get behind in their payments to you.

TAXES

There are many interesting possibilities about this business as far as taxes are concerned. The important thing to remember starting out is to keep very good records of any purchases and any expense you incur: seeds, plants, pots, soil, plastic bags, labels, invoices, etc. Your watering cost and delivery costs are deductible, of course. Home-based businesses can have many other tax advantages, but that's another very complicated subject beyond the scope of this book. Suffice to say that it's definitely worth looking into with a tax accountant.

OTHER BUSINESSES

There are also other businesses that this one can lead to, depending on your time, space, interest and resources. There seems to be an endless market for potted herbs at nurseries and garden centers. Potted herbs are also easily sold at Farmer's Markets all over the country.

Herb growing can also lead you into herb products, such as herb vinegars, dried herb seasoning packets, sachets, herb pillows, etc.

I've found fresh culinary herbs to be the most profitable for me, but it's also possible to include additional sidelines as you learn more about these remarkable plants.

One thing will happen after it becomes known that you have an herb business: you'll soon be considered an "expert" on culinary herbs and will be asked to speak at garden clubs, horticultural societies, garden centers, cooking classes, etc. Its lots of fun and always offers a chance to tell where your fresh herbs are being sold.

HARVESTING, PACKAGING AND KITCHEN USE

PERHAPS you've already noticed in the sales section of this book that I never mention herb packet weights. If you've already started looking at herbs in markets, you've seen that many herbs are sold by weight. Some are sold by the small bundle.

When I started in this business, I wanted to get into it without a lot of start-up costs. I wanted to make sure there really was a good market out there for my herbs before I invested in such costly things as commercial scales and fancy printed labels.

My system worked so well that I still don't use scales, although I did start using printed labels for my herb packets at the end of my second year.

What worked for me can work for you, so what I'm describing is the low cost way to start your own herb business.

PACKAGE AND LABEL

First of all, purchase a package of plastic freezer bags at your super market. As of this writing, my local store sells 80 1-quart capacity bags for about two dollars. They measure 4"x2"x12" and are .95 mil thick.

Then purchase a small package of stick-on labels measuring approximately 2½"x3" or 3"x4". There are many sizes available. As of this writing, these are for sale at my local drug store for approximately $4 for a package of 150.

The next thing you'll need is a waterproof pen. A laundry pen will work quite well.

These three items are the basic packaging you'll need the first season. It will keep your costs at a few pennies per pack.

Now all you need to add is a little bit of creative thinking about making your first labels by hand. Or maybe you're like I am and panic at the thought of drawing so much as a flower petal. If so, just consider using your rubber stamp.

Your label should say: FRESH HERBS, Company Name, Telephone Number and Address. Be sure to leave lots of white space on the label where you can write in with a waterproof pen the name of the herb. This stamp can also be used for your invoicing.

The address and phone number give customers a chance to reach you and that kind of identification is usually necessary under the law.

Make your labels and stick them onto the bags just before you harvest. Write the herb name on the label before you fill the bag. Be sure to use a water proof pen.

I'm including a picture of my own herb label to give you an idea when you do go to print labels. But I would advise against printed labels the first year. Well grown herbs will sell easily with hand made labels and you should concentrate your first year on learning the business and taking money in. Spending money is easy. Learn the fun of going into your local markets to sell them something instead of always buying. I'm also including a picture of a hand made label like the one I used the first year.

The one problem with these labels is the expense: nearly ten cents each in quantities of less than a thousand or so. That's why I don't recommend them for beginning herb growers. Keep your expenses as low as possible the first year while you make sure this little business is the right one for you. Make your first labels by hand, or with a rubber stamp. Printed labels can come later.

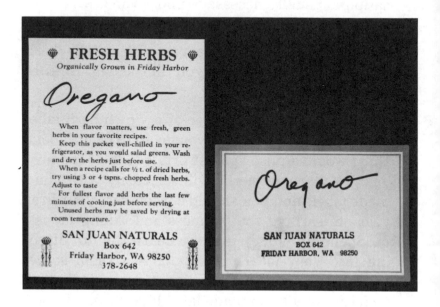

This is the label I now use in my herb packets. It's known as a "crack & peel" label, and is quickly applied, easily stored and looks good in the produce market. The ink is dark purple. Easy handmade label on the right.

HOW AND HOW MUCH TO PICK

So now your first crop of herbs is ready to be harvested and taken to the greengrocer. What follows is an herb by herb description of harvesting and packaging for market. Because we're not using a scale, some of the descriptions of how much to pick may seem a little vague. You must always look at what you're doing with one eye for the customer. Is the person who buys your little herb packet going to feel that they are getting good value for their money? By now you will have checked out several markets where herbs are sold and know if you're giving good value in comparison to those herbs.

When herbs are growing well they produce lots and lots of pickable harvest. Be generous in your packaging and you'll never hear any complaints. If you're too skimpy your sales will drop off.

The time of day you pick your herbs is not as important as the fact that they are dry when you pick them. Wet herbs rot quickly in the plastic bags, so time your watering for after harvest. Don't wash your herbs before selling for the same reason. I grow herbs without using herbicides or pesticides on or around them, so I'm not worried about the produce I take to market. I strongly suggest you follow that pattern, too.

But what if, you might ask, you go to the garden and find the lovely dill fronds covered with aphids? Well, it can certainly happen, and since I'm strongly advising against the use of pesticides, I had better give you some solution for such a problem at harvest time. Of course you'd wash off the aphids, carefully and gently in cold water. And I'd definitely urge the use of a salad spinner to dry the herbs after that washing. Even blotting with paper towels is a good idea in order to take the herbs to market dry, so they'll last longer.

Incidentally, I never seal the plastic bags, but leave them open at the top. The smell of fresh cut herbs is a big selling point; with open bags customers can sniff all they like.

If you pick in the heat of the day, don't leave the filled bags in the sun. Place them in your refrigerator until you finish picking the whole order and can take them to market. On hot days, you can take a bucket of ice to the garden. It's very important to keep the herbs cold.

I use my fingers and fingernails to pinch off the stem ends of almost all herbs, but a small knife, or scissors is needed for cutting chive bunches. I kneel on a plastic pad at each plant I'm harvesting and can easily pick 30 or 40 mixed bags of herbs in less than an hour. You'll be slower, of course, to start, but that's mostly because you'll be uncertain of how much to pick.

When you're first learning to package, get hold of a little postage (oz.) scale. (Any one who has ever belonged to Weight Watchers should have one.) I'll give you some approximate weights to start, but the most important point to remember is: How does the bag look?

I am also including some recipe information in this section to try and push you into using more herbs in your own kitchen. That will lead you to more ideas for sales, more enthusiasm in what you are doing.

HARVESTING HINTS

BASIL HARVESTING: The first thing to remember about harvesting this herb is to not let it go to flower. Flower and seed setting on a basil plant stops its leaf production and spoils the plant for harvesting. If flower stems appear, pick them immediately and include them in your packet for market.

A lot of basil is sold by the uprooted bunch, but I prefer to nurse my plants along, picking leaves and stems carefully so that the same plants will produce for me from mid-June through September or even October. I make at least two plantings, but don't abandon the first one when the second is ready to pick. Just go back and forth, one bed to another, letting the plants rest between pickings.

Ten to fifteen basil stems (depending on the leaf size) should make a full looking bag and weigh in at about 2½ ounces.

(All these weights are very approximate, and depend on the size and maturity of the leaves and stems. Your eyes are the best judge of good value.)

BASIL IN THE KITCHEN

This key herb is nearly synonymous with the word Pesto, which itself derives from the word pestle.

Although many different herbs can be used to make delicious herb pastes (pestos) the most common is made with a recipe similar to this one.

Basil Pesto

Put one to two cups of basil leaves in a blender or food processor. Add two to four cloves of garlic, ½ to a full cup of parsley leaves. Blend and chop thoroughly and add ¾ cup good olive oil slowly. Also add ½ cup grated Parmesan cheese and ¼ cup pine nuts or walnuts. (The nuts are optional.) Blend all into a thick sauce. This sauce is perfect over any cooked pasta or noodles. It is a fine addition (a tablespoon at a time) to any salad dressing; a tasty spread for sliced tomatoes (add Italian cheese and French bread for a super sandwich). Indeed, basil pesto can be used to flavor any vegetable, baste any barbecue, or be used any time great flavor is needed. Just make it and taste — you'll think of new ways to use it yourself.

DILL HARVESTING: Here's another reminder to be sure you're growing the ferny or tetraploid dill. Ten or twelve stems of mature ferny dill should weigh in at about 1½ ounces and make a fine looking package. When the plants are quite young, perhaps fifteen stems would be needed. Just make the package look good for a cook, who can dry any extra dill not needed immediately. It will keep well for quite a while in the refrigerator.

DILL IN THE KITCHEN

Fresh green dill leaves can be used in place of dill seeds in almost any recipe. It is extra nice for use in salads, in yoghurt or sour cream dips, and in the cooking of fish, especially salmon.

Dill Mayonnaise Salmon

Put salmon filets or steaks on a cookie sheet and cover the top with dill fronds. Spread a mixture of mayonnaise and dijon mustard over the fish. (Use one tablespoon of mustard for each ½ cup mayo.) Broil the fish about three inches from the heat until fish flakes easily with a fork.

FRENCH TARRAGON HARVESTING: It takes almost half the season in my area for the tarragon bed to really produce well, so I only sell a few bags a week until early July. Then I bale out the tarragon to markets and restaurants while it's at the peak of production. Ten to twelve stems will make a good looking bag and should weigh about 1½ ounces.

FRENCH TARRAGON IN THE KITCHEN

What a tasty, anise-like addition to so many dishes. Excellent with chicken, eggs and fish, tarragon is also an excellent seasoning for potatoes, spinach, peas and cauliflower.

Tarragon Chicken Salad

2 cups diced cold chicken
1 cup finely chopped celery
1 cup green grapes cut in half
¾ cup mayonnaise
1 Tablespoon chopped tarragon
Combine all ingredients and mix gently but thoroughly. Let stand one hour in the refrigerator before serving.

Tarragon bed in early summer

THE SCARBOROUGH MIX: This herb mix often outsells all but basil in my market accounts, and I seriously recommend it for you. Its a fine way to gain new customers who can try several herbs at once. It also makes a good herb mix at home chopped in salads, soups, etc.

In the bottom of the plastic bag, place six or seven fluffy sprigs of curly parsley, then add three or four stems of sage, three or four stems of thyme leaves (and flowers) and two or three stems of rosemary.

Mark the label: Parsley, Sage, Rosemary and Thyme and, if you're generous with your parsley, it will be a lovely, fragrant packet of useful herbs that many people will buy.

MINT HARVESTING: I probably fill my mint bags fuller than any others because mint is occasionally for sale rather cheaply and I want my customers to feel they're getting a big bag full of mint from me. I only use stem ends with perfect leaves (not snail eaten or moldy) and I fill the bag almost to the top. Try fifteen or even twenty stems and the bag might weigh 2+ ounces. I often use mixed mint varieties and mark the bag MINTS.

MINTS IN THE KITCHEN

Too often seen as a mere garnish for iced tea, fresh mint can easily become a basic herb in your kitchen. Here are a couple of ideas to get you started taking mint a little more seriously in your own kitchen.

Zucchini with Mint

Grate or finely chop 6 or 8 small zucchini and saute in 3 tablespoons melted butter.
Add ¼ cup chopped spearmint or peppermint and saute for a minute or two.
Salt and pepper to taste. Serves 3 or 4.

Garbanzo Spinach Salad

1 large or 2 small heads spinach
1 can 16 oz. garbanzo beans
1 cup diced celery
½ cup raisins
¼ cup chopped mint leaves
Wash, dry and chop spinach
Add washed, drained garbanzo beans, celery, raisins and chopped mint. Dress with vinaigrette.
(see p. 54). Serves 4 to 6.

OREGANO HARVESTING: *This can be a little tedious to pick as Greek oregano is somewhat smaller and slower growing than the more common variety. But the Greek variety is very desirable for cooks so I do strongly recommend it. In harvesting, try twelve to fifteen stem ends weighing approximately 1½ ounces. Add a few flower stems and blossoms, if there are any.*

MARJORAM HARVESTING: It can be harvested much as the oregano, and weighs about the same. When the knotted flower stems start, add a few stems to each packet for fragrance, looks and taste.

OREGANO & MARJORAM IN THE KITCHEN

These herbs can be used interchangeably and together.

Simple Spaghetti or Pasta Sauce

4 cups chopped fresh tomatoes
1 cup chopped onion
¼ cup olive oil
3 Tablespoon chopped oregano leaves
2 tablespoon chopped marjoram leaves
Salt to taste

Put all ingredients together in a sauce pan and simmer twenty to thirty minutes. Serve over pasta with grated Parmesan cheese.

Herb Butter

A delicious seasoning for French Bread.
½ cup sweet butter
¼ cup finely chopped marjoram, oregano
and basil leaves

Whip together in a food processor or blender. Spread on sliced french bread before or after heating, or at the table. For extra flavor, add 1 clove garlic.

FRENCH SORREL HARVESTING: As your sorrel bed develops, you'll have small, medium and large leaves. The largest leaves may need folding to fit in the bag. Once a plant gets overgrown with very large leaves, I cut it back completely so that new, more tender leaves will grow. The flavor is often better from smaller leaves. Don't include stems in your sorrel bags; they are not edible and take up too much space. I

Fresh sorrel leaves after cutting tall stems.

Cut tall sorrel flower stems for better leaf production.

fill a sorrel bag completely, much as I do for mint. A full bag of sorrel may weigh as much as three ounces or more.

As I have mentioned before, the important thing to remember with sorrel is to keep the seed stalks cut back as soon as they appear.

FRENCH SORREL IN THE KITCHEN

For an easy beginning with this distinctive herb, try some sorrel leaves in your next tuna salad — maybe one fourth as much sorrel as lettuce.

Then try sorrel leaves chopped into your next cole slaw. Sorrel has the ability to make ordinary everyday foods taste a little bit extraordinary.

Sorrel Soup

3 tablespoons butter
2 or 3 medium potatoes
2 cups washed, chopped sorrel
1 cup chopped onion
3 cups chicken stock
1 cup milk

Saute the onions until quite wilted, then add the chopped sorrel and saute another minute or two. Meanwhile, wash, peel and slice the potatoes. Add them to the pan with the onions plus the chicken stock. Bring to a boil and simmer for 25 or 30 minutes until the potatoes are tender. Put through a blender or processor. Return to the pan. Stir in milk and reheat if you are serving the soup hot, or chill it to serve cold. Do not bring it to a boil after adding milk.

ROSEMARY HARVESTING: At least eight or ten stems of rosemary are needed per bag when you're selling rosemary by itself. The weight would be approximately one ounce. But its a slow growing plant in most weather zones, so you may not have a lot of rosemary to offer your first year. In fact, it is probably a good idea to use it exclusively the first year or two in the Scarborough Mix. If you live in a very warm sunny climate, you can sell lots and lots of it all the time.

ROSEMARY IN THE KITCHEN

Oven Fries with Rosemary

Cut three baking potatoes into 8 wedges each. Place potatoes in an oiled oven-proof dish and pour ½ cup good olive oil over all. Then sprinkle with 2 tablespoons chopped rosemary. Cover the dish and cook for about 20 minutes at 350 degrees. Remove from oven, uncover, turn the potatoes, turn up the oven to 425 degrees and cook for another ten minutes or so until the potatoes are golden brown and quite tender. The outside should be a little crispy. Cook them until they are. Serves 4 or 5.

Beets with Rosemary

This can be made with fresh or canned beets; fresh herbs can jazz up even the most mundane of foods. Cook and slice fresh beets, or open a can of sliced beets. Drain the liquid into a saucepan (or save the cooking liquid.) Add ½ cup any flavorful vinegar (wine, fruit or cider), ¼ cup sugar and three good rosemary sprigs; cut from the tips. Boil for a few minutes and then pour over the beets in a bowl. Chill before serving.

CHIVE HARVESTING: When harvesting chives, even for your own use, be certain to cut them off close to the bottom of the plant. Snipping the tip ends of chive plants is wrong. Circle a bunch of chives, about three inches in diameter, with your left hand and, holding it firmly, cut through the greens an inch from the ground.

The first cutting or two, the chives will be clean and ready to place in the plastic bag. However, after a few harvests they become "dirty" with weeds and stiff flower stems, etc. When you cut these "dirtier" chives you should then hold the cut bunch close to the tips and shake them. All the junk should drop out. Trim off any yellow tips (from previous cuttings) and make the chives look as perfect as possible. The packet weight should be about three ounces.

If available, its nice to include a stem or two of chive buds in each packet.

I also sell chive flowers in my markets; they are edible fresh in salads and are delicious dipped in Tempura batter and fried. This is handy when you end up with as many chive plants as I do. See the following recipe.

Chive harvesting.

Shake the stems to loosen weeds and debris.

CHIVES IN THE KITCHEN

There's no way to use up all the chives you're going to be growing; just remember to add them chopped to soup, salad, vegetables or omelets. They are perfect, of course, for chive butter or in sour cream. Eight or ten chive stems chopped up into a tuna salad will lift it right up into a special class.

Chive Blossoms in Tempura Batter

Wash chive blossoms gently but thoroughly. (Tiny insects love to hide in all flower blossoms.) Dry the blossoms by use of a salad spinner or by shaking dry in a colander. Make tempura batter with 1 cup cake flour, 1 cup ice water, 1 egg, ¼ teaspoon baking powder and ¼ teaspoon salt. Stir gently, then add another ⅓ cup (approx.) cake flour to blend in with only one or two strokes. Set the batter bowl in ice water as you're working. The batter should be lumpy. Dip the washed, dry chive blossoms in the batter, three or four at a time, and fry in peanut oil at 375 degrees for about two minutes — or until golden brown. Use a wok if you have one.

THYME HARVESTING: It takes quite a few sprigs of thyme to make a decent package; perhaps eight or nine multi-stemmed sprigs. I also usually include a few thyme flowers. They are pretty, edible and add to the look of the packet. The approximate weight of a thyme packet might be one ounce. Don't cut and package woody stems. Only the tender green stems are edible.

Harvest thyme stems, leaves, flower buds and blossoms.

THYME IN THE KITCHEN

The most common uses of fresh thyme are in *bouquet garnis* (tied up herbs to season soups and stocks) and as a key ingredient in clam chowder.

But, used in moderation, thyme leaves can add zip to all sorts of soups and salads, any long, slow cooked meat dish, and I like the flavor in sauted or braised onions.

Sauteed Onions with Thyme

Slice one pound onions while melting 3 or 4 tablespoons of unsalted butter in a pan. If the thyme is tender stemmed, add 2 tablespoons finely chopped leaves and stems. If the stems are woody, roll the stems between your hands to strip off the tiny flavorful leaves. Let the thyme cook for two or three minutes in the butter, then add the sliced onions, stir and cook for at least twenty or thirty minutes until the onions start to brown. This is a wonderful side dish to go with roasted or barbecued meats.

SAGE HARVESTING: Although used primarily in the Scarborough Mix, a few packets of sage do sell. Try fifteen to twenty tip ends in a packet and add a flower stem or two when available. The packet should weigh about 1½ ounces.

I must stress one last time that you let your eye be your guide on this harvesting. Try to deliver packets that look both perfect (no brownish tips, no bits of weed or dirt) and very generous. Follow these two rules and you will be successful, no matter what your packets weigh.

SAGE IN THE KITCHEN

It almost seems worth growing a sage plant just to have it for Thanksgiving dressing and to garnish the turkey platter. But there are some other uses you may like; it is very good in bread, corn bread and biscuits. Give these biscuits a try and see what you think.

Sage Biscuits

2 cups flower
3 teaspoons baking powder
1 teaspoon salt
2 tablespoons fine minced sage leaves
⅓ cup oil
⅔ cup milk

Mix the dry ingredients into a bowl, make a hole in the center and add the liquid. Stir only until it's well mixed. Drop by heaping tablespoons onto a greased cooking sheet and bake in a preheated oven (450 degrees) for 10 or 12 minutes until the tops are lightly browned.

AFTERWORD

THERE ARE two last bits of information to exchange before the end of this book.

The first one is for me to let you know that the very best (most) money to be made in herbs (after you have a well established, well producing garden) is through a restaurant distributor. These are the people who can call you up once, twice or three times a week and order fifty to three hundred packets of herbs for their next delivery to the best restaurants in the region.

But you must have a large, very steady supply before they will be willing to deal with you. Work toward that goal if you possibly can. Even though that's a bit beyond the scope of this book and quite a few more herb plants are necessary, it is certainly worth working towards and it can be handled in EXACTLY the same way as far as growing, harvesting, packaging, etc. You may have to make a few price changes to be more competitive at that point (with herb suppliers of other areas) but it can still be very, very rewarding.

And by the time you get to that level, you'll know a lot more about how to operate a more profitable business.

That leaves your input to me as the very last subject. This effort is a first for me and I'm anxious to know what I left out, what I should make more clear, how you're doing, what questions you have, etc.

If this book is a success, I'll keep revising it and adding more information. I'd love to have your ideas and suggestions for the next edition.

This is a business that can happen all over the country; every small town can support at least one fresh herb grower. I'd like to hear from those who try it. And perhaps be even more helpful to those who follow after.

Good luck and kindest regards,

Lee Sturdivant
Box 642
Friday Harbor, WA 98250

August, 1988

REFERENCE BOOKS

E VERY bookstore and library now offers several choices on books about herbs, their cultivation and use. I'd like to recommend a few to get you into the subject and then you can count on your own enthusiasm to carry you along.

HERB BOOKS

HERBS. How to Select, Grow and Enjoy by Norma Jean Lathrop, HP Books, 1981.

This is an excellent introductory book in a large paperback format that I consider the best available for beginners in herb gardening. The photos alone are worth the reasonable price and the text is quite a good one. If you've never grown herbs, take a look at this book first.

GROWING AND USING HERBS SUCCESSFULLY by Betty E.M/ Jacobs. Garden Way Publishing, 1976.

One of the few herb books that deals with any commercial efforts for small herb growing businesses. Excellent help for growing parsley and chives commercially. Lots of information in this one for propagating herbs by stem cuttings — something you may want to learn to do.

HERB GARDENING AT ITS BEST by Sal Gilbertie with Larry Sheen. Atheneum, 1978.

This book is especially helpful in fitting herbs into your landscape; how you can start an herb garden from scratch without a lot of previous gardening knowledge and how the plants will behave for the first year or two. It shows how herbs grow above and below ground, so you can get some idea of how the plants will do in your garden.

THE RODALE HERB BOOK edited by William H. Hylton. Rodale Press, 1974.

A big rambling hunk of a book with endless information, both relevant and not-so relevant, but fascinating to the serious herb grower. The contributors are all the gardeners who got in and learned a lot about herbs before they began to be so popular. Don't rush out and buy it until you see if you're really going to "get into" herbs, but once you're there you will want to add it to your library.

RODALE'S ILLUSTRATED ENCYCLOPEDIA OF HERBS. Rodale Press, 1987.

Their updated herb book, easier to use than the one listed above, full of pictures, drawings, chef tips and a broad listing of common and unusual herbs from Agrimony to Zatar.

HOW TO GROW MORE VEGETABLES by John Jeavons, 10 Speed Press, 1979.

A good introduction to intensive gardening practices, spacing, etc.

THE COMPLETE BOOK OF HERBS AND SPICES by Sarah Garland. Viking Press, 1979.

Originally published in England, this is a superior book for herb identification because the botanical water colors and photographs are truly outstanding. If your interest should go far beyond the basic culinary herbs, this book is for you. Lots of interesting recipes, with an English flavor from savory pudding to wassail bowl.

HERBS. GARDEN, DECORATIONS AND RECIPES by Emile Tolley and Chris Meade. Clarkson, Potter Publishers.

Put this one on your Christmas wish list. Its spendy and elegant, but it gives a marvelous full color treatment of herbs at their highest and best use. The photographs alone will make you see herbs in a whole new way and the recipes, though not simple, are inspiring.

THE FORGOTTEN ART OF FLOWER COOK-ERY by Leona Woodring Smith. Pelican Publishing 1985.

COOKING WITH FLOWERS by Zack Hanle. Irene Chalmers Cookbooks, Inc.

POISONOUS PLANTS by Lucia Woodward. David & Charles Publishers 1985.

THE SALAD GARDEN by Joy Larkcom. Viking Press 1984.

HERB COOK BOOKS

HOW TO COOK WITH HERBS, SPICES AND FLAVORINGS by Doris Townsend, HP Books, 1982.

THE HERB BOOK by Arabella Boxer and Phillipa Back, Octobus Books, 1980.

COOKING WITH HERBS by Susan Belsinger and Carolyn Dille, Van Nostrand Reinhold, 1984.

COOKING WITH HEALTHFUL HERBS by Jean Rogers, Rodale Press, 1983.

THE HERB AND SPICE COOKBOOK Sheryl and Mel London. Rodale Press, 1986.

SEED AND NURSERY SOURCES

Herb Gathering, Inc., 5742 Kenwood, Kansas City, MO 64110.
One source of Greek oregano seeds. N/C for catalog.

Nichols Garden Nursery, 1190 N. Pacific Highway, Albany, OR 97321.
N/C for Catalog. Source of elephant garlic.

Richters, Goodwood, Ontario, Canada LOC 1AO.
They ship both plants and seeds to U.S. An excellent selection of every possible herb seed, although their seed packets are a little skimpy. $1 for catalog.

Stokes Seeds, Inc., Box 548, Buffalo, NY 14240.
Generous packets of basic herbs. Very helpful instructions on the packets; a fine company to do business with. N/C for catalog.

Taylor's Herb Gardens, 1535 Lone Oak, Vist, CA 92083.
Large selection of herb plants. They ship all over the country all year long. Catalog $0.50.

Well Sweep Herb Farm, 317 Mt. Bethel Rd, Port Murray, NJ 07865.
Plants and seeds. Catalog $1.00.

Geo. W. Park Seed Co., Cokesbury Rd, Greenwood, SC 29647.
Herb plants and seeds available. N/C for catalog.

HERB MAGAZINES AND ORGANIZATIONS

The Business of Herbs
Box 559
Madison, VA 22727

Herb Business Bulletin
P.O. Box 32
Berryville, Arkansas 72616

Herb Quarterly
Newfane,
VT 05345

Herb Society of America
2 Independence Ct.
Concord, MA 01742

INDEX

Basil 14-17, 85, 86
Bergamot 47
Billing details 74, 75
Borage 47
Cabbage 52, 54
Calendula 47
Carnations 47
Chard 52
Chervil 41
Chicory 51
Chives 32-33, 98-101
Chrysanthemums 47
Cilantro 41
Citrus 48
Climate zones 13
Daylillies 48
Dianthus 47
Dill 18-19, 87
Edible flowers 43-49
Elephant garlic 42
Endive 52
English daisy 48
Farmer's market 73
Fennel 42
Fertilizer 59
Food demonstration 71-72
French tarragon 21-22, 88
Fuchsia 48, 52
Geranium 48
Gladiolus 48
Harvesting 79-106
Hollyhock 48
Improving your sales 71-74
Intensive gardening 12
Invoice 76

INDEX

Kale 52
Label 80-82
Lavender 48
Lilac 49
Lovage 42
Marigold 49
Marjoram 26-22, 92
Marketing 63-70
Mint 22-23, 90
Mixed herbs 51
Nasturtiums 49, 53
Oregano 24-25, 91-92
Oriental greens 52
Other businesses 78
Packaging 79
Pansy 49
Parsley 34-35, 54, 89
Pesticide 59
Restaurant accounts 70
Rose 49
Rosemary 30-31, 89, 96-97
Sage 38-39, 89, 105
Scarborough mix 89
Seed starting 55-58
Shallots 42
Sorrel 28-29, 93-95
Squash blossoms 49
Store accounts 63-66
Summer savory 42
Sweet marjoram, see marjoram
Taxes 72
Thyme 36-37
Toxic blossoms 50
Vinaigrette 54
Viola 49

ORDER FORM

San Juan Naturals
Box 642S
Friday Harbor,
Washington, 98250

Please send _____ copies of **PROFITS FROM YOUR BACKYARD HERB GARDEN** at $10.95 each.

I understand that I may return the book for a full refund if not satisfied.

Name _____

Address _____

City _____ State_____ Zip _____

Washington State Residents: Please add 7% Sales Tax.

Shipping $1 for first book and 50c for each additional book.
_____I can't wait for Book Rate. Here's $3 per book for Air Mail.